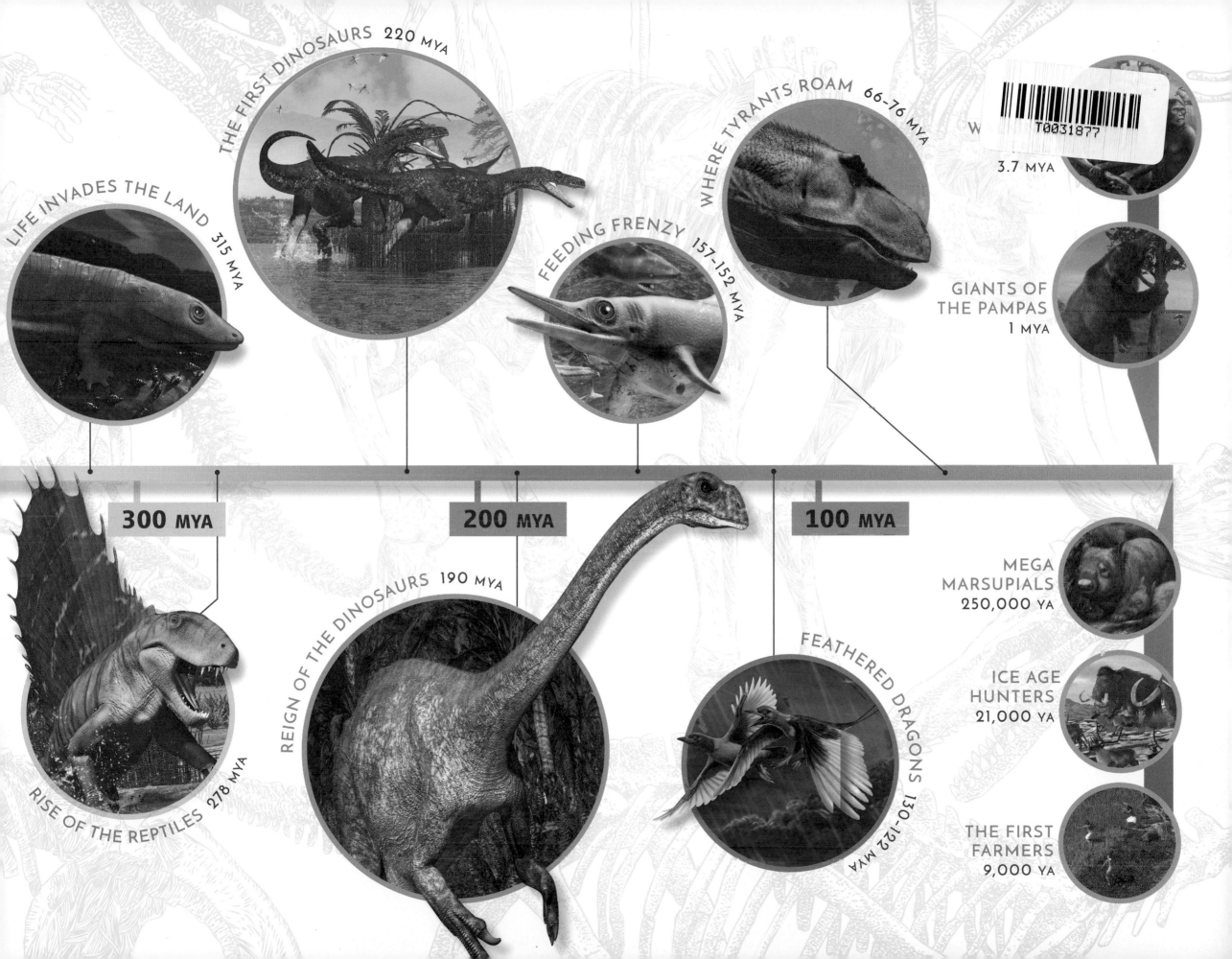

LIFE INVADES THE LAND 315 MYA

THE FIRST DINOSAURS 220 MYA

WHERE TYRANTS ROAM 66-76 MYA

FEEDING FRENZY 157-152 MYA

3.7 MYA

GIANTS OF
THE PAMPAS
1 MYA

300 MYA

200 MYA

100 MYA

RISE OF THE REPTILES 278 MYA

REIGN OF THE DINOSAURS 190 MYA

FEATHERED DRAGONS 130-122 MYA

MEGA
MARSUPIALS
250,000 YA

ICE AGE
HUNTERS
21,000 YA

THE FIRST
FARMERS
9,000 YA

LIFE THROUGH TIME

THE 700-MILLION-YEAR STORY OF LIFE ON EARTH

WRITTEN BY
JOHN WOODWARD

CONSULTANT CHRIS BARKER

DK LONDON
Senior Editor Carron Brown
Senior Art Editor Sheila Collins
US Editor Kayla Dugger
Production Editor Kavita Varma
Production Controller Sian Cheung
Senior Jacket Designer Suhita Dharamjit
Managing Editor Francesca Baines
Managing Art Editor Philip Letsu
Publisher Andrew Macintyre
Associate Publishing Director Liz Wheeler
Art Director Karen Self
Publishing Director Jonathan Metcalf

Illustrators James Kuether, Davide Bonadonna, SJC Illustration, Jon Hughes, Sofian Moumene, Claudia Saraceni/The Art Agency

First American Edition, 2020
Published in the United States by DK Publishing
1450 Broadway, Suite 801, New York, NY 10018

Copyright © 2020 Dorling Kindersley Limited
DK, a Division of Penguin Random House LLC
21 22 23 24 10 9 8 7 6 5 4 3 2
008–317629–Sep/2020

A catalog record for this book
is available from the Library of Congress.
ISBN 978-0-7440-2017-5

DK books are available at special discounts when purchased in bulk for sales promotions, premiums, fund-raising, or educational use. For details, contact:
DK Publishing Special Markets,
1450 Broadway, Suite 801, New York, NY 10018
SpecialSales@dk.com

Printed and bound in China

For the curious
www.dk.com

MIX
Paper from
responsible sources
FSC™ C018179

This book was made with Forest Stewardship Council™ certified paper - one small step in DK's commitment to a sustainable future. For more information go to www.dk.com/our-green-pledge

CONTENTS

3   LIVING SEAS

4   AN EXPLOSION OF LIFE

6   AGE OF FISHES

8   LIFE INVADES THE LAND

10   RISE OF THE REPTILES

12   THE FIRST DINOSAURS

14   REIGN OF THE DINOSAURS

16   FEEDING FRENZY

18   FEATHERED DRAGONS

20 WHERE TYRANTS ROAM

22   WALKING TALL

24   GIANTS OF THE PAMPAS

26   MEGA MARSUPIALS

28   ICE AGE HUNTERS

30   THE FIRST FARMERS

32   EVOLVING EARTH
      AND INDEX

LIVING SEAS
Ediacaran period 635-541 million years ago

Long before there was life on land, organisms were evolving in shallow seas. Their fossils, found in the Ediacara region of South Australia, show they had more complex bodies than the tiny, simple living things that came before them. But we do not know how they lived, or even if they were animals. Some, like *Kimberella*, may have crept over the seabed to graze on bacteria. Others, such as *Charnia*, were anchored in the mud and probably filtered the water for food.

Charnia

Funisia

Dickinsonia

Spriggina

Kimberella

Marrella was a small animal with a hard, segmented external skeleton. It had a spiny shield extending over its head and long antennae.

Waptia was similar to a shrimp, with a shell-like outer covering over the front part of its body and a segmented tail.

A simple branched sponge, *Vauxia* lived by filtering food particles from the water.

Rooted to the spot like a coral, *Echmatocrinus* used its crown of tentacles to gather food.

AN EXPLOSION OF LIFE
Cambrian period 508 million years ago

High in the Rocky Mountains of British Columbia, Canada, a rock formation called the Burgess Shale preserves the fossils of animals that lived on a muddy seabed more than 500 million years ago. They were part of the "Cambrian explosion" of different life forms, which resulted in a variety of animals that still exist—plus many others that have completely disappeared.

Marrella

Pikaia

Opabinia

Echmatocrinus

Wiwaxia

One of the strangest Burgess Shale animals, *Opabinia* had five eyes and a long trunk ending in a "toothed" grabbing part.

Wiwaxia slid over the seabed on a sluglike foot, so it may have been an early mollusk. Its back was protected by scales and long spines.

Named after the country in which it was found, *Canadia* was a bristly, segmented worm similar to a modern ragworm.

The free-swimming, eel-like *Pikaia* may have been an ancestor of vertebrates (animals with a backbone), such as fish.

Anomalocaris was a powerful predator with spiky, prey-seizing mouthparts.

Yohoia swam just above the mud, using its spiny arms to catch prey.

Canadia

Waptia

Nectocaris

Anomalocaris

Vauxia

Yohoia

Hallucigenia

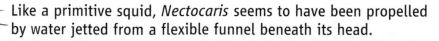

Like a primitive squid, *Nectocaris* seems to have been propelled by water jetted from a flexible funnel beneath its head.

Hallucigenia walked on soft, flexible legs like those of a living velvet worm. It had seven pairs of sharp defensive spines.

Anemones attached themselves to rocks and used their stinging tentacles to catch small animals, dragging them into their bodies to be digested.

Ammonites were multitentacled relatives of the squid and octopus, protected by strong shells. They could swim freely, buoyed up by gas in their shells.

AGE OF FISHES
Devonian period 419–359 million years ago

The Devonian saw the rapid evolution of fishes into many different types, shapes, and sizes. They included the armored placoderms, some of which were huge, powerful fish with bone-crunching bites. Other fish, like *Cladoselache*, were the ancestors of modern sharks and rays. The seas also teemed with shellfish and other invertebrates such as ammonites, trilobites, anemones, and corals.

Stethacanthus

Sponge

Cladoselache

A swift, agile fish-hunter, the shark *Cladoselache* would have been preyed upon in turn by the giant placoderm *Dunkleosteus*.

 *Stethacanthus* was a sharklike fish with a strange structure on its dorsal fin, which possibly protected it from predators.

 Trilobites were flattened, segmented animals that lived mainly on the seabed. There were many more trilobites in earlier ages.

Bothriolepis was a placoderm fish armored with bony plates. It lived near the seabed, feeding on edible debris.

Sponges were abundant in Devonian seas. Like modern sponges, they lived by straining food from seawater pumped through their bodies.

Crinoids, or sea lilies, gathered food from the water while anchored to the seabed by strong stalks. Relatives of starfish, they still exist today.

Ammonite

Dunkleosteus

Bothriolepis

Crinoid

Rugose coral

Trilobite

Dunkleosteus was a colossal armored placoderm, up to 20 ft (6 m) long. It had bladelike teeth for slicing through prey.

Rugose corals had crowns of soft tentacles for snaring prey. Ridges on their conical, stony skeletons were left by stages in their growth.

Like all amphibians, *Dendrepeton* lost vital body moisture easily and had to live in damp places.

Insects such as Brodia—similar to a modern dragonfly—had already taken to the air. Some insects had wingspans of up to 28 in (70 cm).

LIFE INVADES THE LAND
Carboniferous period 315 million years ago

Until about 470 million years ago, complex life existed only in the oceans. But then plants began sprouting on land, to be followed by the ancestors of centipedes, spiders, and insects. Fossils found in the rocks of Nova Scotia, Canada, show that by 315 million years ago, these animals were living in steamy swamp forests of giant trees—where they were preyed upon by salamanderlike amphibians and the first reptiles.

Plants such as *Calamites*—a type of horsetail—flourished in the swamp forests. Their dead remains would turn to coal over millions of years.

Calamites

Brodia

Dendrepeton

Graeophonus

 The spiderlike whip scorpion *Graeophonus* preyed on smaller animals, seizing them with a pair of spiny, pincerlike body parts called pedipalps.

 The *Dendropupa* snails seen here swarming over a *Lepidodendron* trunk were among the earliest-known land snails.

 The huge millipede *Arthropleura* could grow to 8 ft (2.5 m) long. It lived on the forest floor, where it fed on plants and edible debris.

Protoclepsydrops was possibly one of the earliest synapsids—the line of vertebrates that eventually gave rise to mammals.

Lepidodendron

Arthropleura

Protoclepsydrops

Dendropupa

Hylonomus

Lepidodendron trees with diamond-patterned bark grew to 98 ft (30 m) high. The branches were covered in fine, needlelike leaves.

 *Archerpeton* belonged to a group of amphibianlike creatures often called microsaurs. It hunted insects and similar animals.

 One of the first scaly reptiles, *Hylonomus* had waterproof eggs that could be laid out of water in dry places.

Gigantic insects thrived in the Permian climate. One griffinfly—similar to a dragonfly—was the size of a crow.

Chunky *Diadectes* was one of the first big land animals to become specialized for eating tough, chewy plants.

Cypresslike *Walchia* trees provided welcome shade in the hot, dry climate of the time.

The sail-backed *Edaphosaurus* was a plant-eater, despite resembling the predatory *Dimetrodon*.

RISE OF THE REPTILES
Permian period 278 million years ago

During the Permian period, the climate became drier, but in parts of what is now North America, there were small rivers and lakes inhabited by a spectacular variety of animals. They included many types of reptiles that had evolved over the past 25 million years. They lived alongside amphibians and reptilelike synapsids—the ancestors of mammals.

Walchia

Edaphosaurus

Diadectes

Dimetrodon

Casea

The big stomach and digestive system of the synapsid *Casea* show that it was adapted for eating plants.

Armed with a mouthful of serrated, meat-slicing teeth, the big synapsid *Dimetrodon* was the most powerful predator of its time.

Although a predator itself, *Seymouria* would have been easy prey for a far more powerful *Secodontosaurus*.

The predatory *Secodontosaurus* had a spectacular spiny sail on its back, like its relative *Dimetrodon*. Its purpose is not known.

Eryops, an amphibian, had a huge mouth for scooping up big prey and swallowing it.

The strange boomerang-shaped head of the amphibian *Diplocaulus* may have helped it swim.

 Labidosaurikos was a plant-eating reptile, with multiple rows of teeth for grinding fibrous leaves into an easily digested pulp.

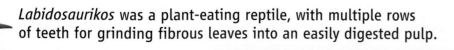 A slender, lizardlike reptile with a long tail, *Araeoscelis* probably preyed mainly on insects, spiders, and similar small animals.

The heavyweight mammal ancestor *Placerias* had two stout tusks and a parrotlike beak, used to tear at juicy plant stems and leaves.

Coelophysis was a slender, probably fast-running dinosaur that would have used its speed to catch and eat smaller lizardlike reptiles.

The big plant-eater *Desmatosuchus* had stout defensive armor and long shoulder spines.

Relatives of dinosaurs, pterosaurs were flying reptiles with leathery wings like those of bats.

THE FIRST DINOSAURS
Triassic period 220 million years ago

Some 252 million years ago, a mass extinction wiped out most of life on Earth, but we do not know why. Life recovered slowly during the Triassic period that followed, but by 220 million years ago, new types of animals were thriving. They included mammal ancestors, early flying pterosaurs, formidable crocodilelike reptiles, and the first small, mainly meat-eating dinosaurs.

Pterosaur

Coelophysis

Placerias

Desmatosuchus

Smilosuchus

Koskinonodon

The aquatic amphibian *Koskinonodon* would have been a patient predator, waiting to seize anything that swam near its jaws.

Distantly related to crocodiles but a lot bigger, *Smilosuchus* probably lurked in ambush for prey like *Koskinonodon*.

 Although it looked like a dinosaur, *Postosuchus* was more closely related to crocodiles. It was the most powerful predator of its time.

One of the earliest dinosaurs, *Chindesaurus* was a hunter, but it would have been wise to avoid much bigger killers like *Postosuchus*.

Postosuchus

Chindesaurus

Drepanosaurus

Trilophosaurus

Arganodus

Xenacanthus

Tree-climbing *Drepanosaurus* probably dug insects out of dead wood with its claws.

An eel-like freshwater shark, *Xenacanthus* had a long spine on its head to protect it from attack.

Arganodus was an early lungfish—a type of fish that can survive drought by burrowing into mud and gulping air into its lungs.

 Easy prey for a hunter like *Postosuchus*, the lizardlike *Trilophosaurus* had big, sharp-edged teeth for slicing tough plants.

 *Dilophosaurus* was a hunter armed with sharp, serrated teeth. It had a double crest on its snout that it used for display.

 Long-tailed pterosaurs like *Rhamphinion* evolved and flourished in the Triassic, and the Jurassic skies were still ruled by these flying reptiles.

REIGN OF THE DINOSAURS
Jurassic period 190 million years ago

The Jurassic period saw the dinosaurs become the dominant animals on land. Here, the animals in a dry region of what is now the US are gathering to drink at a tree-lined pool. Among the dinosaurs and soaring pterosaurs are some extinct relatives of animals that still exist today, including ancestors of crocodiles and mammals.

Ferns and other simple plants carpeted the ground. There were no flowering plants.

Cycads spread their palmlike leaves in the Jurassic sunshine. Similar plants live today in warm regions.

Cycad

Fern

Coelophysis

Dilophosaurus

 Predatory crocodilelike reptiles such as *Calsoyasuchus* lived in much the same way as modern crocodiles.

 *Kayentatherium* was a small, furry animal that was a relative of modern mammals. It was probably a good swimmer.

 Lean, lightweight, and agile, the small meat-eating dinosaur *Coelophysis* was a very successful predator.

Scelidosaurus was a plant-eating dinosaur. Its skin was armored with bony plates for defense against hunters such as *Coelophysis*.

Rhamphinion

Tree fern

Araucaria

Scelidosaurus

Calsoyasuchus

Sarahsaurus

Scutellosaurus

Kayentatherium

 Araucaria trees, or monkey puzzles, were among the most common conifer trees in the Jurassic.

Tree ferns grew in the shade of the big trees and were eaten by plant-eating dinosaurs.

 The dog-sized *Scutellosaurus* was a small, armored relative of the much bigger, heavier plated dinosaur *Stegosaurus*.

 *Sarahsaurus* was a long-necked plant-eating dinosaur related to gigantic, heavyweight sauropods like *Diplodocus*.

15

 A sleek, elegant hunter, the shark *Hybodus* had a tough spine in front of its dorsal fin for defense against bigger predators.

Streamlined, fast-swimming *Brachypterygius* was an air-breathing reptile that would have had to swim to the surface to breathe.

The stout, blunt teeth of the fish *Lepidotes* could crush clams and similar prey.

Lepidotes

Thrissops

Dakosaurus

Ammonite

Hybodus

Brachypterygius

Bait ball

The bony fish *Thrissops* was a fast-moving hunter, like modern tuna or barracuda.

FEEDING FRENZY

Jurassic period
157–152 million years ago

While giant dinosaurs roamed the land in the late Jurassic, the oceans were ruled by predatory marine reptiles. They patrolled seas that teemed with life, from armored mollusks, such as ammonites, to fish whose only defense from attack was to crowd together in a tight, swirling shoal.

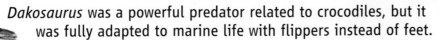 *Dakosaurus* was a powerful predator related to crocodiles, but it was fully adapted to marine life with flippers instead of feet.

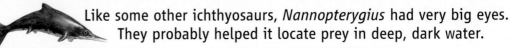 Like some other ichthyosaurs, *Nannopterygius* had very big eyes. They probably helped it locate prey in deep, dark water.

 The remains of *Dacentrurus*, a drowned dinosaur in this scene, would eventually sink to the seabed to be buried among the bones of marine life. The terrifying jaws of the gigantic *Pliosaurus* enabled it to attack and eat very big prey—including other marine reptiles.

The flying pterosaur *Rhamphorhynchus* may have dived to catch fish like a modern seabird.

Sleek, squidlike belemnites used their hooked arms to seize prey.

The plesiosaur *Kimmerosaurus* is named after the rock containing fossils of all these animals—Kimmeridge Clay in England.

Plesiochelys was related to early sea turtles. It lived in shallow coastal seas and probably preyed on jellyfish and similar animals.

17

An early, feathered relative of the gigantic *Tyrannosaurus*, *Yutyrannus* was a powerful hunter that may have targeted *Dongbeititan*.

Birds like *Confuciusornis* flew around the heads of the giant dinosaurs. Males had extra-long tail feathers.

Dongbeititan was a sauropod—a long-necked giant that could reach high into the treetops to feed.

Repenomamus was one of the biggest mammals of its time. It preyed on small dinosaurs.

Yutyrannus

Confuciusornis

Dongbeititan

Repenomamus

Horsetails

Psittacosaurus

Psittacosaurus had a row of quill-like bristles extending down its tail and was a much smaller ancestor of the mighty horned dinosaur *Triceratops*.

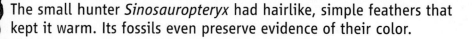

The small hunter *Sinosauropteryx* had hairlike, simple feathers that kept it warm. Its fossils even preserve evidence of their color.

A plant-eater related to early "duck-billed" dinosaurs, *Bolong* could rear up on its strong hind legs to browse on tree foliage.

The lizard *Xianglong* was able to glide from tree to tree on "wings" of skin that were supported by extended ribs.

FEATHERED DRAGONS
Cretaceous period 130–122 million years ago

Until recently, most of the dinosaur remains known to science were of bones and teeth. But fossils discovered in Liaoning, China, in the early 1990s showed that many of the meat-eating dinosaurs had feathers. This proved that they were closely related to birds, and in fact many bird fossils were found in the same rocks. They lived alongside several much bigger dinosaurs, as well as pterosaurs and small mammals.

Xianglong

Ginkgo

Beipiaosaurus

Bolong

Gladocephaloideus

Sinosauropteryx

Early types of ginkgo tree—a plant still found growing wild in China—were common in the forests of the time.

The dinosaur *Beipiaosaurus* probably ate plants. It was covered in feathers and had huge claws.

Birds shared the skies with pterosaurs like *Gladocephaloideus*, which probably used its long, toothed jaws to snatch fish from the water.

The chicken-sized *Mei* was a slender, feathered, birdlike hunter. Its fossilized remains were found curled up as if asleep.

Tyrannosaurus was a formidable predator, with massively powerful jaws and teeth for biting straight through the bones of its victims.

The "duck-billed" dinosaur *Kritosaurus* had hundreds of grinding teeth for chewing up tough plants.

Flowering plants such as magnolias evolved in the Cretaceous period, alongside insects, including bees, which could pollinate them.

Quetzalcoatlus

Tyrannosaurus

Edmontosaurus

Torosaurus

Juvenile Tyrannosaurus

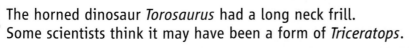

The horned dinosaur *Torosaurus* had a long neck frill. Some scientists think it may have been a form of *Triceratops*.

Quetzalcoatlus was a huge pterosaur with a 33-ft (10-m) wingspan. It was able to soar for hours, but probably hunted on the ground.

Alamosaurus was one of the biggest land animals that has ever lived—a gigantic plant-eating titanosaur with a huge appetite.

The hadrosaur *Edmontosaurus* was similar to *Kritosaurus* but a lot bigger. The deadly *Tyrannosaurus* preyed on this plant-eater.

WHERE TYRANTS ROAM
Cretaceous period 76-66 million years ago

Some of the most spectacular dinosaurs evolved toward the end of the Cretaceous period, just before the great extinction that ended the Mesozoic era—the "age of dinosaurs." In North America, they included giant bone-crunching hunters like *Tyrannosaurus* and huge pterosaurs the size of small aircraft. They shared their world with a wide variety of plant-eating dinosaurs and other animals.

Kimbetohia

Alamosaurus

Deciduous tree

Kritosaurus

Polyglyphanodon

Deciduous trees that replace their broad, thin leaves each spring became common during the Cretaceous, but only in regions with cold winters.

 The lizard *Polyglyphanodon* was one of many that lived alongside the dinosaurs. Some dinosaurs preyed on lizards.

 *Kimbetohia* was a small squirrel-like mammal that probably climbed trees in search of food and to escape enemies.

Cercopithecoides, a relative of modern colobus monkeys, lived in the trees on the fringes of the grasslands, eating leaves as well as juicy fruits.

The biggest savanna animal was *Deinotherium*, a giant relative of modern elephants with huge tusks that sprouted from its lower jaw.

Sivatherium was a short-necked, heavyweight relative of giraffes. It ate both leaves and grass.

Antelopes like these oryx roamed the savannas, targeted by hyenas and other hunters.

Deinotherium

Sivatherium

Cercopithecoides

Giraffe

Oryx

Australopithecus afarensis

Known as *Australopithecus afarensis*, these distant ancestors of human beings would have behaved more like apes but may have used simple tools.

Ostriches were common on the open grasslands. Their long legs gave them the speed they needed to outrun their enemies.

Life was dangerous on the open plains, leading to the evolution of animals that could run fast, such as the horse *Eurygnathohippus*.

Ancylotherium was a big horselike animal with very long front legs, giving it the height to gather leaves from trees.

WALKING TALL
Pliocene epoch 3.7 million years ago

In 1976, archaeologists working in Laetoli, Tanzania, found humanlike footprints in an ancient layer of volcanic ash. The prints are the earliest graphic evidence of distant ancestors that could walk upright. They lived at a time when a drier climate led to the expansion of savanna grassland and the evolution of new types of fast-running animals.

Vulture

Ostrich

Ancylotherium

Termite mound

Dinofelis

Hyena

Eurygnathohippus

Python

The tall trees were browsed by giraffes very similar to the ones that still live in Africa.

Hyenas prowled the plains. They were dangerous enemies of our early ancestors.

Heavy-bodied pythons lurked among the rocks. They killed by coiling around prey and squeezing until it could not breathe.

The leopardlike *Dinofelis* had extra-long canine teeth for killing big prey. It was one of the most powerful predators of its time.

Deer such as *Antifer* were common on the Pampas grasslands. Like the deer that live there today, males had impressive antlers.

The elephant-sized ground sloth *Megatherium* could reach into the treetops to pull down leaves with its claws while sitting on its tail.

Flocks of ostrichlike rheas roamed the open grassy plains, just as they still do today.

South American foxes would have scavenged scraps from the kills of bigger, more powerful hunters.

Megatherium

Notiomastodon

Smilodon

Toxodon

Antifer

Fox

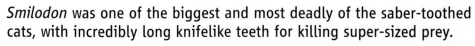

Smilodon was one of the biggest and most deadly of the saber-toothed cats, with incredibly long knifelike teeth for killing super-sized prey.

A heavyweight hoofed plant-eater that weighed more than a ton, *Toxodon* was perfect prey for the saber-toothed *Smilodon*.

Bigger than a grizzly bear, the short-faced bear *Arctotherium* probably had the muscle to steal the prey of a saber-toothed cat.

The *Notiomastodon* would have lived a life very similar to that of the modern elephant, using its long, mobile trunk to gather leaves and grass.

GIANTS OF THE PAMPAS
Pleistocene epoch 1 million years ago

Some 2.5 million years ago, the world entered a series of ice ages that saw vast ice sheets spread over northern continents. In South America, however, the region we now call the Pampas was a grassy plain inhabited by a variety of giant mammals. These "megafauna" included outsized relatives of modern armadillos, giant ground sloths, and fearsome predators.

Arctotherium

Rhea

Glyptodon

Macrauchenia

Skunk

Tapir

Skunks relied on their foul-smelling defense to protect them from enemies.

The tapirs that rooted in the undergrowth were very like those that still live in South America.

The size of a small car, *Glyptodon* was a heavily armored mammal with a massive skull and big grinding teeth for chewing tough grass.

A big, camel-like plant-eater, *Macrauchenia* had a long neck that allowed it to browse in the trees, as well as crop the grass at its feet.

Palorchestes was a relative of modern wombats, but the size of a horse. Its long claws probably helped it gather leafy food.

The enormous goanna lizard *Megalania* was a powerful predator. Males may have fought over females like modern Komodo dragons.

Genyornis was a big, flightless bird with massively powerful legs, similar to an emu.

Macropus titan was a close relative of today's gray kangaroo.

Palorchestes

Megalania

Saltwater crocodile

Thylacine

Macropus titan

Sarcophilus

MEGA MARSUPIALS
Pleistocene epoch 250,000 years ago

Isolated from all other continents for 30 million years, Australia has evolved its own distinctive forms of wildlife. The native mammals are nearly all marsupials—animals that carry their undeveloped young in pouches. Around 250,000 years ago, these included some spectacular giants that lived alongside many animals that we can recognize today.

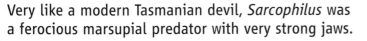

Very like a modern Tasmanian devil, *Sarcophilus* was a ferocious marsupial predator with very strong jaws.

Once widespread across Australia, the thylacine was the marsupial equivalent of a wolf. The last one died in 1936.

As big as a rhinoceros, the giant wombat *Diprotodon* was the largest marsupial—and Australian mammal—that has ever lived.

 Related to the giant wombat, *Zygomaturus* probably lived in wet places, where it used its long lower teeth to dig up water plants.

Diprotodon

Zygomaturus

Procoptodon

Koala

Thylacoleo

Progura

Wonambi

Echidna

Hairy-nosed Wombat

The giant short-faced kangaroo *Procoptodon* could reach up 10 ft (3 m) into trees to eat leaves.

The biggest Australian predatory mammal of its time, *Thylacoleo* had a crushing bite.

 Like modern mallee fowl, *Progura* laid its eggs in a mound of dead vegetation that heated up as it decayed, keeping the eggs warm.

 Similar to a python, *Wonambi* could grow to a length of 20 ft (6 m). It would have no trouble swallowing a wombat whole.

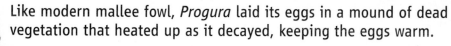

Golden eagles soared over the grassy plains searching for prey, just as they do today in remote parts of the north.

Some of the Ice Age people living on the steppe built houses from the huge bones of dead mammoths, covering them with animal skins.

ICE AGE HUNTERS
Pleistocene epoch 21,000 years ago

At the peak of the Ice Age, ice covered large regions of northern continents. The ice sheets were fringed by treeless, half-frozen tundra, but beyond that lay vast areas of dry grassland known as the mammoth steppe—home to a spectacular variety of animals, including the magnificent woolly mammoth.

Golden eagle

Steppe bison grazed in herds, very like those that still survive in North America.

Wild horses flourished on the plains, using their speed to escape danger.

Camp

Steppe bison

Musk ox

Wild hors

Saiga antelope

Woolly rhinoceros

 As big as a modern white rhino, the woolly rhinoceros had a shoulder hump filled with energy-rich fat that helped it survive the winter.

 Musk oxen lived in small herds on the tundra, where they were preyed on by Arctic wolves, much as they are today.

Covered in long hair to keep out the Ice Age chill, the woolly mammoth had long, spiral-curved tusks and was the size of an African elephant.

 The cave lion was the most feared predator of its time. It probably lived in prides like an African lion, hunting together for big prey.

Raven

Cave lion

Woolly mammoth

Reindeer

Humans

Ravens used their strong bills to pick at the remains of dead animals.

Herds of reindeer roamed the plains, shadowed by wolves and human hunters.

 Adapted for life on cold, dry grasslands, saiga antelope ranged across the entire mammoth steppe from the UK to Siberia and Alaska.

 The people living at this time were just like us, but used stone tools and weapons. They wore clothes made of animal fur to keep warm.

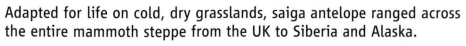

The earliest towns were dense clusters of houses, lived in by people who either farmed or made goods that they could trade for food.

As well as growing crops, people would have gathered food from the wild. These native palm trees provided juicy, sweet dates.

THE FIRST FARMERS
Holocene epoch 9,000 years ago

As the world warmed up at the end of the Ice Age, people living in the Middle East discovered that they could gather the seeds of wild plants and use them to grow crops such as wheat. They were the first farmers. By 9,000 years ago, they were producing enough to support whole communities of people with different trades, who built the first towns.

Town

Palm tree

Wild boar

Deer

Crane

Stout fences

Fish were an important part of the early farmers' diet and often dried for eating later.

Before the invention of pottery, people used animal skins to carry water back to their homes.

Wild animals such as deer were common. Deer were a problem because they ate crops, but they were also a source of food.

The farmers used hand tools such as picks, hoes, and sickles made of deer antlers or wood with sharp-edged flint blades.

Wild boar, deer, and other animals were hunted using stone-tipped spears and arrows, just as they had been for thousands of years.

People would have hunted big birds such as these cranes, and in spring they probably raided their nests for eggs.

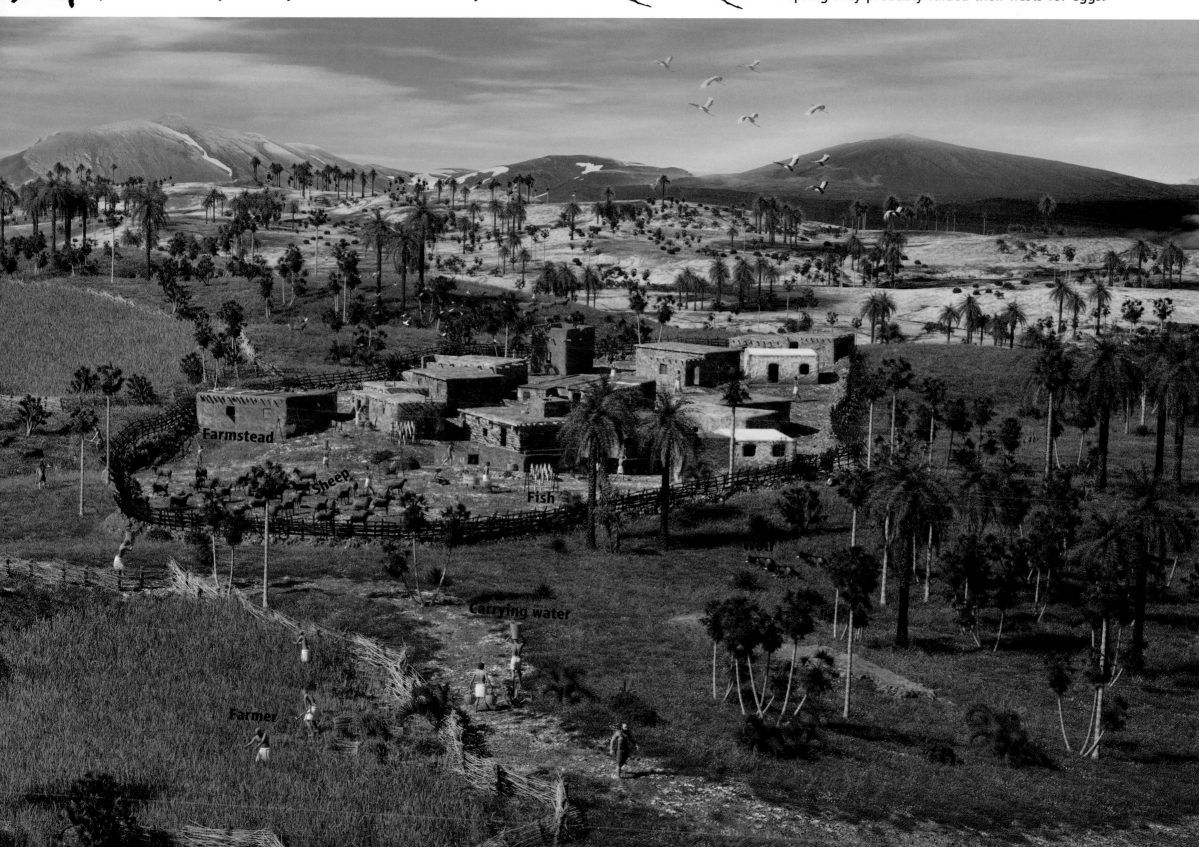

Farmstead

Sheep

Fish

Wolf

Carrying water

Farmer

The farmsteads were made up of simple square mud-brick buildings with flat roofs.

Dangerous predators such as wolves were a constant threat to early farmers.

Fields would have been enclosed by stout fences to stop wild animals such as deer and gazelles eating the precious crops.

Sheep were among the first animals to be domesticated. Shepherds watched over them as they grazed to protect them from wolves.

31

Evolving Earth

Throughout the long evolution of life, the planet itself has been changing too. Massive forces beneath its crust have relentlessly dragged continents around the globe, pushing them together and ripping them apart. This process has redrawn the map over and over again, creating a series of worlds that were very different from the one we live in today.

500 MYA

500 million years ago (MYA), there were two main continents, both tropical: Laurentia and Gondwana. But there was little life on land at this time.

420 MYA

As life began to colonize the land, Laurentia was becoming larger and moving closer to the smaller Baltica. Siberia had formed and was moving north.

380 MYA

By the Devonian "age of fishes," Laurentia and Baltica had collided to form Euamerica, though Siberia was still an isolated continent.

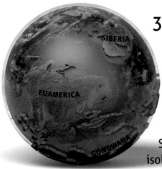

300 MYA

Plant and animal life were flourishing on land when Eurasia merged with the southern continent Gondwana to form the main part of the supercontinent Pangea.

220 MYA

When the first small dinosaurs were evolving, all the continents had pushed together to create one giant supercontinent with a desert at its heart.

180 MYA

Pangaea started splitting apart during the Jurassic period, when dinosaurs dominated on land. This created new versions of Laurasia and Gondwana.

120 MYA

As the first flowering plants bloomed, Laurasia and Gondwana drifted apart. Each continent started splitting up, forming the beginnings of the modern world.

80 MYA

Toward the end of the Mesozoic "age of dinosaurs," the Atlantic opened up, separating America from the Old World. High sea levels flooded most of north Africa.

50,000 YA

At the height of the most recent ice ages, the world map looked much like it does today, but low sea levels had turned many shallow seas into dry land.

Index

ammonites 6, 8
amphibians 8, 10, 11, 12
anemones 6
antelopes 22, 29
Australia 3, 26–27

bears 25
birds 18, 19, 22, 24, 26, 27, 28, 29, 31
Burgess Shale 4–5

Cambrian period 4–5
Canada 4–5, 8–9
Carboniferous period 8–9
cats
  Dinofelis 23
  Smilodon 24
China 18–19
Chindesaurus 13
coal 8
Coelophysis 12, 14, 15
Confuciusornis 18
continents 32
corals 6, 7
Cretaceous period 18–21
crinoids 7
crocodiles 26
  relatives of 12, 13, 14, 15

deer 24, 29, 30, 31
Devonian period 6–7, 32
dinosaurs 12, 13, 14–21, 32

Ediacaran period 3
eggs 9, 27, 31

elephants, relatives of 22, 25
  mammoths 28, 29
England 16–17

farming 30, 31
feathers 18, 19
fish 5, 6–7, 13, 16, 30
footprints 23
fossils 3, 4, 8, 17, 18, 19
fur 14, 29

Glyptodon 25

Holocene epoch 30–31
horses 23, 28
humans 28, 29, 30, 31
  ancestors of 22, 23
hyenas 23

ice ages 25, 28–29, 32
ichthyosaurs 16
insects 8, 10, 20
invertebrates 6

Jurassic period 14–17, 32

Laetoli 23
Liaoning 19
lizards 19, 21, 26

mammals 18, 19, 21, 25, 26, 27
  ancestors of 9, 10, 12, 14
mammoths 28, 29
marsupials 26, 27
megafauna 25
Mesozoic era 21, 32
millipedes 9
mollusks 4, 16
monkeys 22

North America 10, 21
  Canada 4–5, 8–9
  US 12–15

Permian period 10–11
plants 8, 14, 20, 30
  see also trees
Pleistocene epoch 24–29
plesiosaurs 17
Pliocene epoch 22–23
pterosaurs 12, 14, 17, 19, 20, 21

reptiles 8, 9, 10, 11, 14, 17

sauropods 15, 18
sea life 3, 4–5, 16–17
sharks 6, 13, 16
snails 8
snakes 23, 27
South America 24–25
spines (defensive) 4, 5, 12, 13, 16
sponges 4, 6, 7
synapsids 9, 10

Tanzania 23
towns 30
trees 8, 9, 10, 15, 19, 21
Triassic period 12–13
trilobites 6
turtle, relation of 17
tusks 12, 22, 29
Tyrannosaurus 20, 21

US 12–15

vertebrates 5, 9

wolves 28, 29, 31
worms 5

Acknowledgments

Dorling Kindersley would like to thank: **Consultant, pp.30–31** Philip Parker; **DTP Designer** Rakesh Kumar; **Jackets Editorial Coordinator** Priyanka Sharma; **Managing Jackets Editor** Saloni Singh; **Proofreader** Jessica Cawthra.

The publisher would also like to thank the following for their kind permission to reproduce their images: James Kuether pp.6–16, 20–21; Davide Bonadonna pp.2–3, 18–19, 26–27; **SJC Illustration** pp.4–5, 28–29; Jon Hughes pp.24–25; **Sofian Moumene** pp.30–31; **Claudia Saraceni / The Art Agency** pp.22–23. The paleogeography globes on p.32 are derived from original maps produced by **Colorado Plateau Geosystems Inc.** Endpaper images: *Front and Back*: **Getty Images:** MattGrove (Background).

All other images © Dorling Kindersley
For further information see:
www.dkimages.com

TIMELINE OF LIFE

For 3 billion years after life began on Earth, the only living things were microscopic single cells – organisms such as bacteria. But by 600 million years ago (MYA), some colonies of single cells evolved into multi-celled organisms – ancestors of today's animals and plants.

The history of life is recorded in rocks such as fossils. Older rocks lie beneath more recent ones, so each layer represents a span of time. Scientists have named many of these to create a timescale of geological periods. These are subdivided into smaller timespans called epochs.

AN EXPLOSION OF LIFE 508 MYA

700 MYA

600 MYA

500 MYA

400 MYA

LIVING SEAS 635–541 MYA

AGE OF FISHES 419–359 MYA